PREHISTORIC ANIMALS

SEA

MONSTERS

MICHAEL JAY

Raintree

Chicago, Illinois

For information about the publisher:
Raintree, 100 N. LaSalle, Suite 1200, Chicago, IL 60602
Customer Service 888-363-4266
Visit our website at www.raintreelibrary.com

Printed in China and bound in the United States.
07 06 05 04 03
10 9 8 7 6 5 4 3 2 1

Library of Congress Cataloging-in-Publication Data:

Jay, Michael, 1956-
    Sea monsters / Michael Jay.
        p. cm. -- (Prehistoric animals)
Includes bibliographical references and index.
Contents: Life in the sea -- Outside skeletons -- Early fish -- Massive jaws -- Killer sharks -- Sea reptiles -- Ichthyosaurs -- Undersea giants -- Long necks -- Savage survivors -- Back to the sea -- Sea monster words -- Sea monster facts --

Sea monsters summary -- Sea monsters on the web.
    ISBN 1-4109-0010-X (lib. bdg.)
    1. Marine animals, Fossil--Juvenile literature. 2. Fishes, Fossil--Juvenile literature. [1. Marine animals, Fossil. 2. Fishes, Fossil. 3. Prehistoric animals. 4. Paleontology.] I. Title. II. Series: Jay, Michael, 1956-   Prehistoric animals.
    QE766.J39 2004
    566--dc21
                                        2003003654

Acknowledgments
The publishers would like thank the following for permission to reproduce photographs:
pp. 3, 18 (tl), 28 (tl) Gavin Page; pp. 8 (tl), 9 (br), 10, 13, 15 (tr), 16 (bl), 17 (br), 18 (cl), 21 (br), 22, 25, 27 (br), 28 (b), 29 Alpha Archive; all other illustrations John Sibbick

Every effort has been made to contact copyright holders of any material reproduced in this book. Any omissions will be rectified in subsequent printings if notice is given to the publishers.

▲ The *Xiphactinus* lived at the same time as the last of the dinosaurs, about 65 million years ago. See page 10 for more information.

CONTENTS

LOOK FOR THE SEA MONSTER

Look for the plesiosaur logo in boxes like this.
Here you will find extra facts, stories, and other
interesting information.

LIFE IN THE SEA

Experts believe that the first life on Earth began in the seas about 3.5 billion years ago. About 700 million years ago, the oceans were home to animals such as jellyfish and worms.

Mawsonites

▲ One of the first animals on Earth was the *Mawsonites* jellyfish.

Some of the world's oldest animal remains have been preserved in rocks at Ediacara, Australia. This area was once a shallow sea, and about 680 million years ago, its waters were filled with all kinds of animals. These included the *Mawsonites* jellyfish and *Dickinsonia*, a flat wormlike creature that grew to 5 inches (13 centimeters) long. *Mawsonites* floated in the sea, eating particles of drifting food, while *Dickinsonia* crawled on the seabed.

Dickinsonia

Cambrian Explosion

Anomalocaris

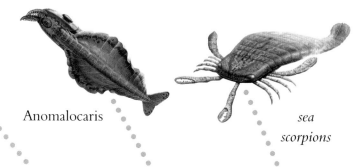

sea scorpions

▶ The story of life in the sea stretches back millions of years. However, most kinds of animals lasted only a few million years before dying out.

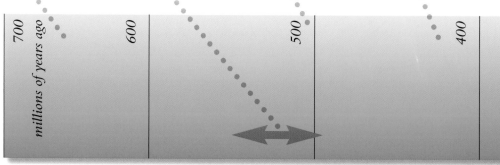

millions of years ago

700

600

500

400

Many new animals appeared later, during a period known as the Cambrian Explosion, and by 500 million years ago the seas were filled with wildlife. Some of these strange-looking creatures were the distant ancestors of today's animals.

▲ The *Anomalocaris* lived about 500 million years ago. The 23-in (60-cm) long hunter had feelers that stuffed prey into its circular mouth.

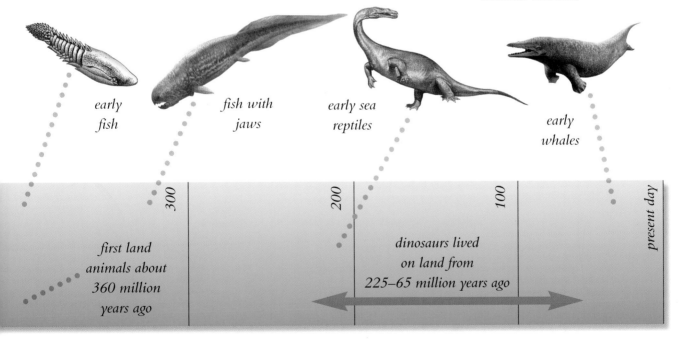

early fish

fish with jaws

early sea reptiles

early whales

300

200

100

present day

first land animals about 360 million years ago

dinosaurs lived on land from 225–65 million years ago

OUTSIDE SKELETONS

Some early sea creatures looked like aliens from another planet. These were arthropods, animals with a hard outer covering instead of a backbone.

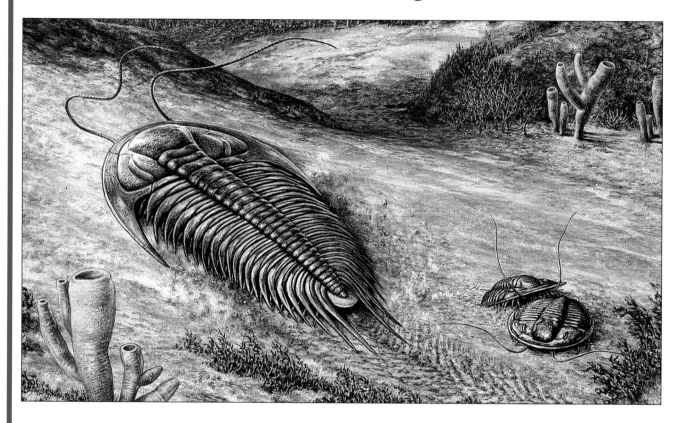

▲ Trilobites are the first known group of arthropods. They lived alongside animals such as sea urchins, corals, and shellfish.

Trilobites were arthropods that lived in the seas about 350–400 million years ago. There were more than 15,000 different kinds. Some were no bigger than a pinhead, while others grew more than 3 feet long.

Trilobites had lots of legs and used these to swim or to walk on the seabed. Trilobites were among the first animals with eyes. Like insects, trilobites had eyes made up of many separate lenses, called compound eyes. A human eye has just a single, large lens.

flattened tail section
called a telson

strong
claws

▲ *Eurypterus* was a fierce but small animal.
It grew to be only about 9 in (10 cm) long.

Some arthropods looked like today's lobsters.
One of these creatures was called the *Eurypterus*.
It was a fierce killer with a long tail, strong
limbs that allowed it to move quickly through
the water or on the ocean floor, and sharp
claws to grab and crush prey.

The *Pterygotus* looked similar but grew
much larger. At 8 feet (2.5 meters) long, it
was the largest arthropod there has ever been.

AMAZING ARTHROPODS

Arthropods were among the
earliest animals and are distant
relatives of modern creatures
such as crabs, lobsters, spiders,
and insects. Today, arthropods
are the world's most widespread
group of animals. There are more
than a million known kinds, but
all share some common features,
including a hard outer skeleton
instead of an inner skeleton. They
also have jointed legs and bodies.

7

EARLY FISH

mouth hole

The first fish had heads covered with bony plates. Most of them were small creatures, and only a few grew more than 8 inches (20 centimeters) long.

The earliest fish are called agnathans, a word that means "without jaws." One of these was a little fish called the *Pteraspis,* shown below. It did not look much like fish today, yet it had several fishlike features.

    Pteraspis had a fin, although this was really a bony spine, one of several along its back. It had a head, but this was made of bony plates, like a helmet. *Pteraspis* also had a mouth, but no moving jaws—instead of biting, it sucked in tiny food particles.

▲ Agnathan fish had a hole instead of a mouth that could open and shut.

Pteraspis *grew about 20 cm long.*

▼ This scene from 400 million years ago shows jawless *Pteraspis* fish swimming along looking for food, such as bits of dead plants and animals.

bony shield around head

eye on each side of wide mouth

fins behind head shield

▲ *Drepanaspis* was a slow swimmer that grew to be 11 in (30 cm) long.

▶ *Hemicyclaspis* had a body that could bend easily.

Other fish that swam in these prehistoric seas included the *Drepanaspis* and the *Hemicyclaspis*. *Drepanaspis* swam along the muddy sea bottom, sucking up food lying there. The *Hemicyclaspis* was a faster swimmer, with fins behind a helmetlike head. Its body was covered with bony strips, which let the 5-inch (13-centimeter) fish wriggle from side to side.

HOW DO WE KNOW ABOUT PREHISTORIC LIFE?

Scientists find out about animals of the distant past by studying fossils, the hardened remains of dead creatures preserved in rock for millions of years. However, only a few animals became fossils. Most were eaten by other animals or decomposed quickly after death. A typical fish fossil was made when a dead fish sank to the bottom of the sea. Sand and silt built up over it, then minerals seeped into the hard, bony parts, changing them into rocky fossil remains.

fossil of a prehistoric sea star

MASSIVE JAWS

Moving jaws were one of the features of later fish, some of which were true sea monsters, growing to enormous sizes.

One of the first really big fish was the *Dunkleosteus*. This monster grew more than 16 feet (5 meters) long, the length of a small truck, and it had jaws packed with jagged bony plates instead of teeth. *Dunkleosteus* could probably swim fast enough to catch most other fish easily. Its razor-sharp tooth plates could slice almost any animal in half.

▶ *Dunkleosteus* lived more than 300 million years ago. Its head had a bony shield.

Xiphactinus *grew about 13 ft (4 m) long*

fish swallowed in stomach

Later fish became more like the fish we see today. They are called teleosts ("complete bones") because they had a full skeleton with a backbone, ribs, and other bones, and were covered with scales. They had powerful tails to drive them forward and special fins that gave precise steering. Teleosts also had a swim bladder. This is an air-filled sac in the body that a fish uses to control its up-and-down movement in water.

THE BIG LUNCH

The *Xiphactinus* was a teleost fish that lived about 65 million years ago, about the same time as the last of the dinosaurs. Its jaws were large and low-slung, much like a present-day grouper fish. The fossilized *Xiphactinus* above may have died of overeating, because the fish it swallowed was too big to digest.

bony tooth plates

KILLER SHARKS

The earliest sharks were fierce hunters that swam in the prehistoric seas about 400 million years ago. Sharks are still deadly ocean predators today.

mouth at front
of head

▲ A *Cladoselache* grew to a length of 6 ft (2m).

▼ The *Stethacanthus* of 360 million years ago had a strange top fin, its purpose a mystery.

One of the earliest known sharks is the *Cladoselache*. This beast hunted the oceans for fish and squid about 360–400 million years ago, long before any dinosaurs walked the earth. At first glance, *Cladoselache* looks similar to a modern shark, but its mouth was at the front of its head (instead of underneath) and its snout was shorter.

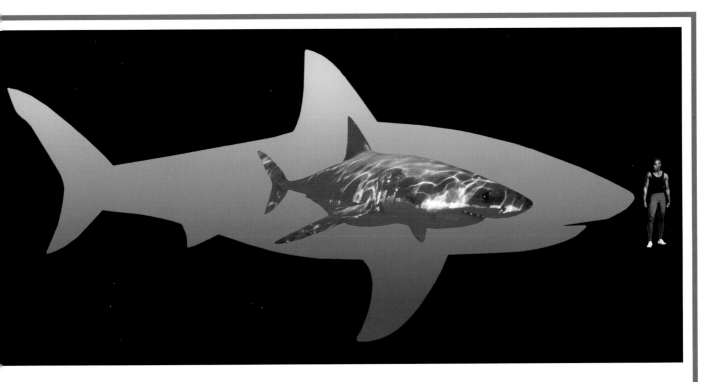

One of the biggest prehistoric sharks scientists know about was the huge *Carcharadon megalodon.* This monster lived about 15 million years ago and grew up to 42 feet (13 meters) long. That makes today's 19-foot (6-meter) long Great White shark seem like a shrimp!

▶ *Carcharadon megalodon* was a huge fish. Here a fossil tooth is shown with a tooth from a Great White shark, today's biggest hunting shark.

▲ *Carcharadon megalodon* compared in size to an adult Great White shark of today, and a human.

Great White shark tooth

Carcharadon megalodon
tooth

GRISTLE INSTEAD OF BONE

Sharks have skeletons of gristly cartilage instead of hard bone. This makes finding shark fossils difficult because early shark remains mostly rotted away in a short time. But their teeth were hard, and this made them more likely to turn into fossils. Many early sharks have been identified by studying the size and shape of their fossilized teeth.

SEA REPTILES

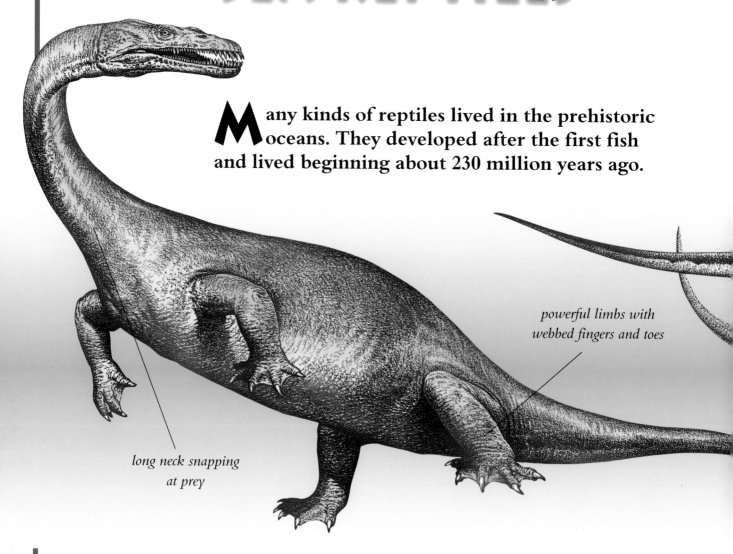

Many kinds of reptiles lived in the prehistoric oceans. They developed after the first fish and lived beginning about 230 million years ago.

powerful limbs with webbed fingers and toes

long neck snapping at prey

▲ There were several kinds of *Nothosaurus.* Like other sea reptiles, they breathed air, not water.

Nothosaurus was a hunter that lived about 220 million years ago. It lived in the water but may also have climbed onto seashore rocks to bask in the sun. It hunted in warm, shallow waters where there were plenty of other animals to chase and eat.

Nothosaurus had long jaws that were packed with dozens of sharp teeth, just right for grabbing and hanging onto a slippery fish trying to escape.

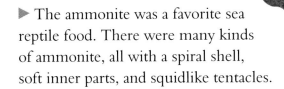

► The ammonite was a favorite sea reptile food. There were many kinds of ammonite, all with a spiral shell, soft inner parts, and squidlike tentacles.

Flippers allowed Ceresiosaurus *to move quickly under water. It lived about 210 million years ago*

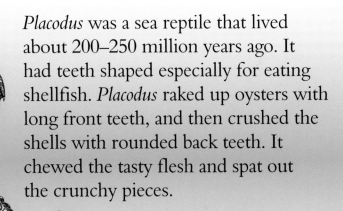

Placodus was a sea reptile that lived about 200–250 million years ago. It had teeth shaped especially for eating shellfish. *Placodus* raked up oysters with long front teeth, and then crushed the shells with rounded back teeth. It chewed the tasty flesh and spat out the crunchy pieces.

front teeth for scraping shellfish off rocks

females probably laid their eggs near the shore

Ammonites were common sea creatures.

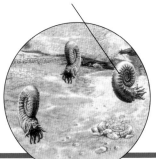

 WHAT IS A REPTILE?

Reptiles were among the oldest animal groups to develop, and they still exist today. Reptiles breathe air and usually have a covering of scales or horny plates rather than fur or hair. They lay tough-shelled eggs on dry land instead of giving birth to live young. They are cold blooded, which means they need warm surroundings to be active.

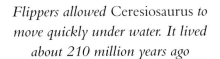

ICHTHYOSAURS

Ichthyosaurs were reptiles, but they looked much like modern dolphins. Ichthyosaurs had long, toothed jaws that could snap up prey such as squid and fish.

Ichthyosaurs were smooth-skinned sea reptiles that swam with sweeping movements of their fins and powerful, sharklike tail. They were rulers of the oceans about 200 million years ago.

Their long jaws and teeth were just right for catching prey, which included various kinds of ammonites and fish. We know about their food because fossilized ichthyosaur droppings have been cut open to show food remains, including ammonite shells and fish bones.

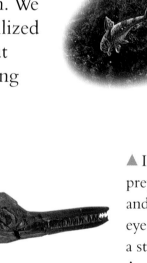

fossil ichthyosaur

▲ Ichthyosaurs found prey mostly by sight and smell. Their big eyes were protected by a strong ring of bones. An ichthyosaur's tail swept from side to side, like that of a fish.

There were many kinds of ichthyosaurs, ranging in size from about 3 feet (1 meter) long to giants that grew to more than 65 feet (20 meters).

WARMER WATERS OF THE PAST

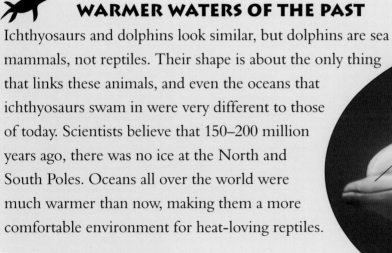

Ichthyosaurs and dolphins look similar, but dolphins are sea mammals, not reptiles. Their shape is about the only thing that links these animals, and even the oceans that ichthyosaurs swam in were very different to those of today. Scientists believe that 150–200 million years ago, there was no ice at the North and South Poles. Oceans all over the world were much warmer than now, making them a more comfortable environment for heat-loving reptiles.

beak and tall fin

UNDERSEA GIANTS

*direction of
water flow*

▲ Pliosaur nostrils had "in" holes and "out" holes. These allowed the pliosaur to detect scents in water as it flowed through.

Other sea reptiles included the plesiosaurs. One group of these were the pliosaurs. These had short necks, chunky bodies, and powerful flippers.

The biggest pliosaur was a meat-eater that ruled the ocean about 150 million years ago. *Liopleurodon* grew to more than 65 feet (20 meters) from nose to tail. It had four massive flippers that allowed it to be a fast, agile swimmer.

Liopleurodon probably hunted mostly by smell, since its nostrils were placed where sea water could flow through them. *Liopleurodon* could sniff scents in the water just as land animals sniff the air for smells.

▲ A complete skeleton of *Liopleurodon* was found in Mexico in 2002. When it was alive, this sea monster could have weighed more than 100 tons.

▶ The *Liopleurodon* was long and sleek, with a skull that measured more than 9 ft (3 m) long.

*human diver to
the same scale as
the main picture*

The tail was too short to be used for forward thrust. The four flippers were used instead.

PREHISTORIC TURTLES

Early turtles included the *Archelon,* a huge sea turtle that lived about 70–65 million years ago. It grew to nearly 13 ft (4 m) long, twice the length of any sea turtle today. *Archelon*'s big shell was made up of a framework of bony ribs that grew out from its backbone. Thick, rubbery skin grew between the ribs, forming the shell's oval shield shape.

Archelon *ate seafood such as shrimp and jellyfish*

Liopleurodon *had a bulky body, but was still very agile.*

Liopleurodon used its flippers to swim, rather than wriggling its tail like a fish or an ichthyosaur. Big muscles gave a powerful downstroke, so it is likely that the flippers were used in pairs, one pair pushing down while the other pair returned for the next push.

front teeth cross over to form fish trap

Liopleurodon *probably ate ammonites as well as sea reptiles, such as ichthyosaurs.*

LONG NECKS

Some plesiosaurs had small heads and long necks. Elasmosaurs were among the biggest of these, with necks that stretched for many feet.

Elasmosaurs are probably the best-known prehistoric sea reptiles. Their long necks had more than 70 bones and were very flexible. An elasmosaur may have fed by poking its head into a school of fish and sweeping its jaws from side to side, snapping up fish one after another. Its flexible neck made this an easy way to go hunting. Adult elasmosaurs grew to more than 45 feet (14 meters) long and swam by making powerful strokes with their pointed flippers.

A MONSTER IN LOCH NESS?

Scientists believe that plesiosaurs, along with most other sea reptiles, died out about 65 million years ago. But some people believe there may be survivors. For hundreds of years, there have been sightings of a "monster" swimming in Loch Ness in Scotland. Loch Ness is nearly 1,000 ft (300 m) deep in places, so there could be room to hide a small colony of plesiosaur-like animals. Scientists have gone on several expeditions to try and find "Nessie." They have used small submarines, cameras, and other high-tech gear, but no proof of these creatures' existence has ever been found.

Elasmosaurs hunted underwater but breathed air, like land reptiles.

Not all plesiosaurs were as big as the huge elasmosaurs. For example, the *Cryptoclidus* was only about 26 feet (8 meters) long, although it still weighed 8 tons.

All plesiosaurs swallowed stones from the ocean floor. By weighing itself down with stones, a plesiosaur could hunt underwater for longer.

▲ Elasmosaur means "plate lizard," named for the wide shoulder bones that carried the front flippers.

▼ *Cryptoclidus* was a smaller plesiosaur. Its jaws were lined with almost 100 teeth.

SAVAGE SURVIVORS

The first crocodiles and alligators lived about 200 million years ago. However, the biggest of all time was the more recent *Deinosuchus*, which lived about 70 million years ago.

▲ A *Deinosuchus* skull is shown here to scale with a dalmatian dog. The skull measured 6 ft (2 m) long, with jaws that were big enough to swallow most prey with a single snap.

The enormous *Deinosuchus* ("terrible crocodile") was a monster that dwarfed any of today's alligators—an adult measured up to 32 feet (10 meters) and weighed 5 tons.

 Deinosuchus probably hunted like alligators and crocodiles do today. It floated just under the surface near the shore, waiting for an animal (such as a dinosaur) to stop for a drink. Then, coming out of the water in a surprise rush, *Deinosuchus* used its enormous jaws to seize its prey and drag it back underwater to eat.

▼ *Deinosuchus*, shown to scale with the much smaller *Metriorhynchus* and a human.

Deinosuchus

Metriorhynchus

human

▲ *Deinosuchus* (foreground) was big enough to snatch a dinosaur as it came to drink.

Metriorhynchus was a crocodile that lived in the sea at much the same time as *Deinosuchus,* but was smaller, growing to only about 9 feet (3 meters) long.

Metriorhynchus was not as heavily armored as other crocodiles and had slim jaws and sharp teeth that could grip wriggling fish or squid. Its tail was not pointed like other crocodiles, but instead ended in a fishlike fin.

THE REPTILE KILLER

Almost all sea reptiles and their relatives, the dinosaurs, died out about 65 million years ago. Scientists believe their deaths were caused by a changing climate and a huge meteor that struck Earth. Alligators, crocodiles, and turtles are among the few sea reptiles surviving today, and alligators now live only in fresh water.

BACK TO THE SEA

There were still ocean giants after the sea reptiles had died out. These were early whales, whose ancestors had been land-dwelling mammals.

The earliest-known whale is the *Pakicetus,* but it looked very different from whales of today. It had four legs and a separate tail, and it probably looked more like a seal than a whale. Compared to other whales, *Pakicetus* was not very big, growing to about 6 feet (2 meters) long. Researchers believe it lived in coastal areas, where rivers met the ocean, about 50 to 55 million years ago.

▶ *Pakicetus* probably spent much of its time paddling in shallow water looking for fish to eat.

nostrils on snout

Pakicetus *was similar to a seal in shape.*

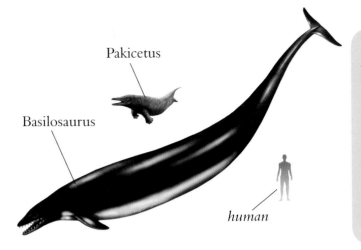

Pakicetus

Basilosaurus

human

▲ *Pakicetus, Basilosaurus,* and a human are pictured here to scale.

ECHOLOCATION

Whales developed a "super-sense" to help them hunt prey underwater. A whale sends out powerful sound waves into the water around it. Echoes that bounce off solid objects, such as edible fish, are received by the whale's sensitive ears, allowing it to have a "sound-picture" of things in the water.

The *Basilosaurus* was a monster whale that came after *Pakicetus,* living about 40 million years ago. At that time, the seas were filled with all sorts of animals. *Basilosaurus* was the biggest of them all, growing to over 65 feet (20 meters) long. *Basilosaurus* was not the only kind of mammal to go back to the sea. The distant ancestors of today's sea mammals, such as the seal, dolphin, and walrus, also once lived on land.

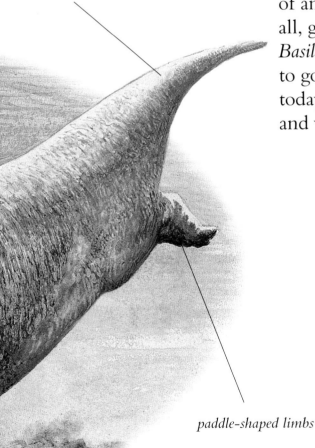

short tail

paddle-shaped limbs

▲ Today's seals live in and around water, yet they are related to land-dwelling weasels.

SEA MONSTER WORDS

◀ *Anglaspis* was a kind of agnathan fish.

Here are some technical terms used in this book.

Agnathan

A general name for very early fish that had no moving jaws. Today's lamprey is a type of agnathan.

Arthropod

Animals that have a segmented body and an outer skeleton, or exoskeleton. Trilobites were prehistoric arthropods. Today, there are more than 1 million kinds of arthropods, including spiders and insects.

Cambrian Explosion

A period in the earth's past when many new kinds of life appeared. It lasted from 540 to 500 million years ago.

Cartilage

A strong but flexible material that some animals have in place of bone. A shark's skeleton is made of cartilage.

Cold-blooded

An animal, such as a reptile or a fish, with a blood temperature that matches the temperature of its surroundings. After a cold night, a reptile warms up in the sun to become active. A warm-blooded animal, such as a whale, has blood that stays the same temperature.

Dinosaurs

A large group of four- and two-legged reptiles that lived all over the world from 225 to 65 million years ago.

Fossil

The remains of a living thing preserved in rock. A "trace" fossil preserves such things as flipper prints left in the mud.

Loch

The Scottish word for lake.

Mammal

A warm-blooded animal, such as a dolphin, whale, or human. Mammals feed their young with milk from the mother's body.

Meteor

Chunks of rock moving quickly in space, ranging in size from tiny grains to flying mountains. A meteor striking Earth is thought to have helped kill off most reptile life on the planet about 65 million years ago.

Plesiosaur

A large group of sea reptiles that had four flippers. Some kinds of plesiosaur had short necks, while others had necks that were long and thin.

Prey

An animal that is hunted by other animals for food. The hunter is called a predator.

Reptile

An animal that breathes air and is usually covered with scales or horny plates. Reptiles normally lay eggs with tough shells on dry land, although ichthyosaurs are thought to have given birth to live young.

Skull

An animal's bony structure that contains and protects its brain, eyes, ears, and nose.

Swim bladder

A small sac inside a teleost fish's body that helps to control its bouyancy.

Teleost

General name for fish with a bony inner skeleton. Teleosts have proved to be the most successful fish—today there are more than 20,000 kinds.

Trilobite

An early arthropod that was among the first animals to have eyes. These were made of many separate lenses (like those of an insect) rather than the single lens that fish and mammals have.

WEIRD WORDS

This pronunciation guide should help you say the names of sea monsters.

Ammonite
ammo-night

Anomalocaris
a-nom-alo-car-is

Archelon
ark-el-on

Basilosaurus
bas-ill-oh-sore-rus

Carcharodon megalodon
car-char-oh-don mega-low-don

Ceresiosaurus
cer-es-ee-oh-sore-rus

Cladoselache
clay-dos-eh-lash

Cryptoclidus
krip-toe-cly-dus

Deinosuchus
dye-no-sook-us

Dickinsonia
dik-in-soh-nee-ah

Drepanaspis
drep-an-asp-is

Dunkleosteus
dun-klee-ost-ee-us

Elasmosaur
el-az-moe-sore

Eurypterus
yer-ip-ter-rus

Hemicyclaspis
hem-ee-sigh-clasp-iss

Ichthyosaur
ik-thee-oh-sore

Liopleurodon
lie-oh-pler-oh-don

Mawsonites
maw-son-eye-teez

Metriorhynchus
met-ree-oh-rink-us

Nautiloid
naw-til-oyd

Nothosaurus
no-tho-sore-rus

Opthalmosaurus
op-thal-moe-sore-rus

Pakicetus
pak-ee-see-tus

Placodus
plah-co-dus

Plesiosaur
ples-ee-oh-sore

Pliosaur
ply-oh-sore

Pteraspis
tear-asp-iss

Pterygotus
terry-goat-us

Stethacanthus
steth-ah-kan-thus

Temnodontosaurus
tem-no-don-toe-sore-rus

Trilobite
try-low-bite

Xiphactinus
zif-act-in-us

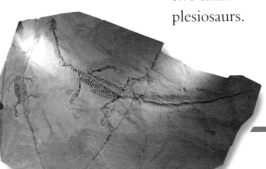

▼ These fossil remains are of two small plesiosaurs.

SEA MONSTER FACTS

▲ These are three kinds of early shark.

Here are some facts and stories about strange sea creatures.

Strange sharks

Some early sharks were truly strange. One had tentacles that grew above its eyes. Another had a forward-facing bony spine above its head, and a third kind had a bony spike growing behind its skull.

► *Opthalmosaurus* grew about 16 ft (5 m) long and weighed about a ton when fully grown.

Fighter jet or airliner?

Researchers have found that short-necked plesiosaurs had wide, stout flippers similar to a fighter plane's wings. This made them very agile and good at chasing fish. Long-necked plesiosaurs had long, slim flippers, like the wings of an airliner, making them suitable for cruising. So it is likely that long-necked plesiosaurs swam slowly over long distances, looking for prey that was easy to catch.

What big eyes you've got

The *Opthalmosaurus* was a common kind of ichthyosaur that had very large eyes. But the eyes of *Temnodontosaurus* were even bigger. One of its fossilized eyes was 10 in (264 mm) across, the size of a dinner plate. All the many kinds of ichthyosaur had eyes that were surrounded by a "doughnut" of bone, called the sclerotic ring. This protected their soft eyeballs when the animal was diving into the deep ocean hunting for squid.

A modern ammonite?

The ammonites died out about 65 million years ago, but the similar-looking nautilus did manage to survive. It is a rare shellfish that lives today in the Pacific Ocean.

First finds

Ichthyosaurs and plesiosaurs have been studied for a long time. Remains were found in Britain more than 300 years ago, and drawings of a bone had been made even earlier, in 1604. A complete ichthyosaur skeleton was found much later, in 1719, and was thought for many years to be the remains of a kind of strange "sea dragon."

Bringing up baby

Female ichthyosaur remains have been found that seem to show they had special places to give birth to young, which were born live rather than as eggs like other reptiles. An ichthyosaur mother could give birth to ten or more live young at a time, although two to three were more common. Babies were born tail-first and were about 19 in (50 cm) long, making them tasty snacks for hungry sharks nearby. The birth places may have been guarded by larger male ichthyosaurs.

▲ Mary Anning was one of the first people to dig up plesiosaur fossils, in England. In 1810 she found her first ichthyosaur when she was just eleven years old.

SEA MONSTERS SUMMARY

The first life began in the seas about 3.5 billion years ago. Remains found in Australia show that about 680 million years ago, jellyfish and worms were living in the water.

After the earliest sea animals, new creatures developed during a period about 500 million years ago, called the Cambrian Explosion. Arthropods had hard, outer shells instead of skeletons inside their bodies. Early fish, called agnathans, had armored heads and fixed jaws. Later fish, called teleosts, had jaws that opened, and scales and fins. Reptiles lived in the seas for millions of years, but they mostly died out about 65 million years ago, at the same time as the dinosaurs. Some land mammals, such as the ancestors of the whale, went to live in the ocean.

▼ This 16-ft (5-m) long sea monster is a nautiloid that lived in the oceans 400 million years ago. Some nautiloids had up to 100 tentacles that grabbed at prey such as trilobites.

SEA MONSTERS ON THE WEB

You can find out about prehistoric sea creatures on the Internet. Use a search engine to type in the name of the animal or the prehistoric period you are interested in. Here are some good sites to start with:

▼ There are good sites that have information on prehistoric sea creatures. Here are three screenshots.

http://www.oceansofkansas.com

The state of Kansas once lay under the sea, and this fascinating site tells you all about life at that time, and other interesting facts.

http://www.museum.vic.gov.au/prehistoric

From ammonites to trilobites, they are all featured on this excellent site.

http://www.sdsc.edu/ScienceWomen

This site features women who have made their names in science, including Mary Anning, the English Victorian-period fossil hunter.

http://www.lymeregis.com/lymefossilshop

Want to buy a fossil? Visit this site to see a treasure trove of bits and pieces for sale.

http://www.bbc.co.uk/dinosaurs

This provides information on the TV series *Walking with Dinosaurs*. It also has material on all sorts of prehistoric sea creatures.

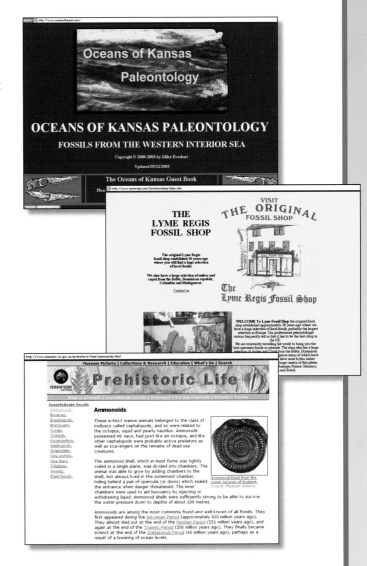

INDEX